MOON

NATIONAL
GEOGRAPHIC

WASHINGTON, D.C.

BY **Steve Tomecek**

ILLUSTRATED BY **Liisa Chauncy Guida**

To my favorite Sky Watchers… Jennifer, Bill, Gavin and Morgan.
Thanks for sharing in my celestial adventures!
—smt

In memory of little Macallan and his daddy Clyde,
Your laughter, humor, and faith will always warm our
hearts when we think of you.
—Your friends & Liisa

The moon always seems to be changing. Sometimes it's big and round. Sometimes it looks like a skinny little banana. Sometimes you can see the moon only at night. Mostly, if you look really hard, you can also see it in the day.

Why does the moon seem to change? What is it made of?
Why does it travel through the sky? Join us as we unlock some
of the secrets of our moon!

The moon looks different from everything else
you see in the sky. It's not as bright as the sun.
It does not hurt your eyes to look at it.
The sun is a star. But the moon
is not a star.

The moon is more like our Earth. The moon is made of rock and gets its heat and light from the hot glowing gases of the sun. If the sun didn't shine on the moon, we wouldn't be able to see it.

A long time ago, many people had strange beliefs about the moon. Some thought that the moon had evil spirits that caused people to act strangely. Some thought that the moon had magic powers and could turn you into a wolf.

When different people looked at the full moon, some thought they could see the face of a "man on the moon." Others thought that the moon was made of green cheese or that strange creatures lived on it.

Back in the year 1609, many of the false ideas about the moon began to change. A scientist named Galileo Galilei used his telescope to take a close-up look at the moon. What he saw surprised everybody.

Galileo discovered that the moon was very much like our Earth. He saw mountains and valleys. He also found out that the large dark patches that made the face on the moon were really large flat areas. He called these large flat areas "seas."

Later on, scientists used much stronger telescopes to discover
that the "seas" were not filled with water like the oceans on Earth.
They were really big holes called craters that were filled with darker
colored rock. Craters form when rocks from space hit the moon.
These rocks, called meteorites, blast holes in the lunar surface.

Meteorites also hit the Earth. But we don't have nearly as many craters as the moon. This is because Earth is surrounded by air and the moon is not. The air helps protect us from many falling space rocks by making them burn up.

Unlike our Earth, the moon has no running water. On Earth, when a crater forms, wind and rain fill it up with loose dirt and small rocks. Since there is no water to fill a crater on the moon, once they form, they last a very, very long time.

Scientists think that some of the craters on the moon are billions of years old. In fact, the only thing that can erase a crater on the moon is another crater. When a new meteorite hits the moon's surface, it blasts out a new crater and some of the rock and dust from the hole actually fills up other older craters.

Looking at the moon from Earth, it seems to be about the same size as the sun. The truth is, the moon is much smaller than the sun.

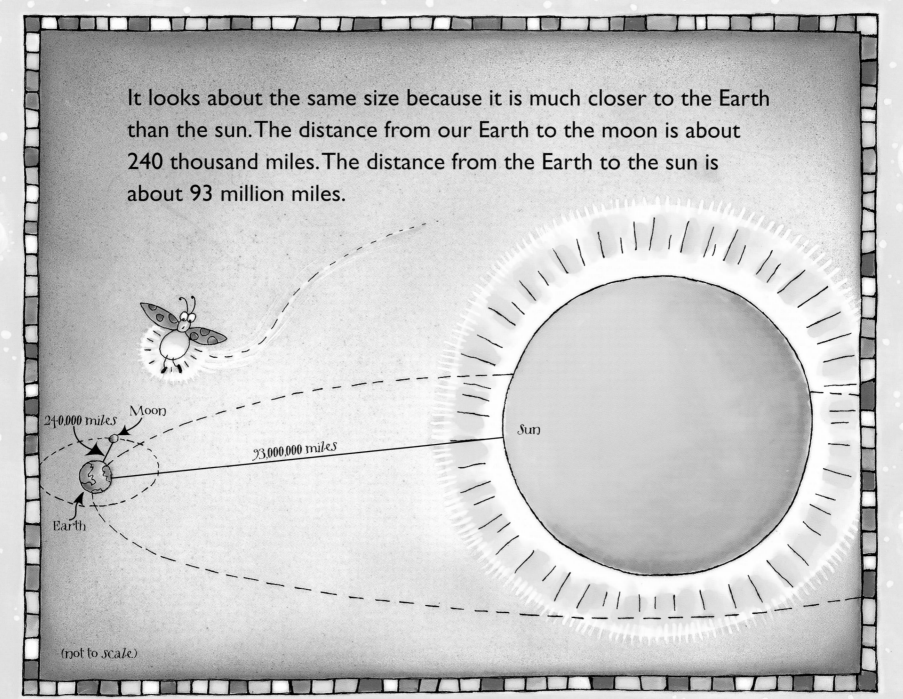

It looks about the same size because it is much closer to the Earth than the sun. The distance from our Earth to the moon is about 240 thousand miles. The distance from the Earth to the sun is about 93 million miles.

240,000 miles Moon

93,000,000 miles

Sun

Earth

(not to scale)

If you could measure the moon across its center, you would find that it is 2,160 miles across.

Our Earth is almost four times bigger than the moon.
It is almost 8,000 miles across.

The moon is our closest neighbor in space. As the Earth travels around the sun, the moon travels around the Earth. The path that the moon takes is called an orbit.

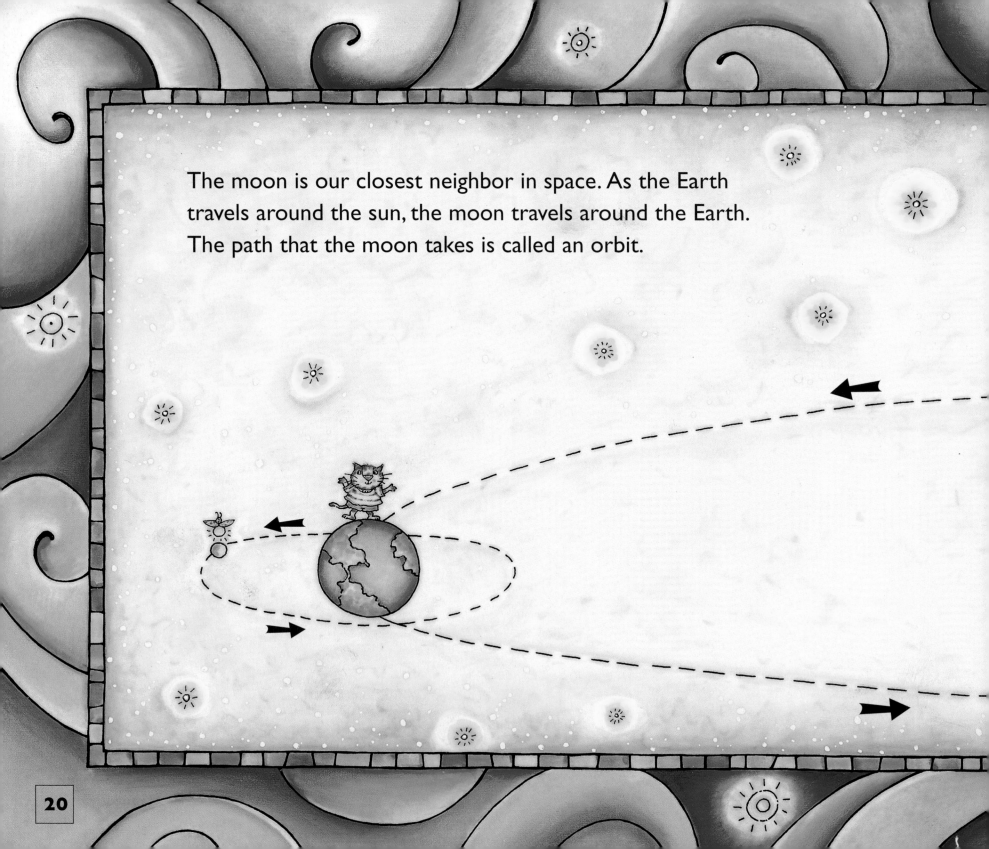

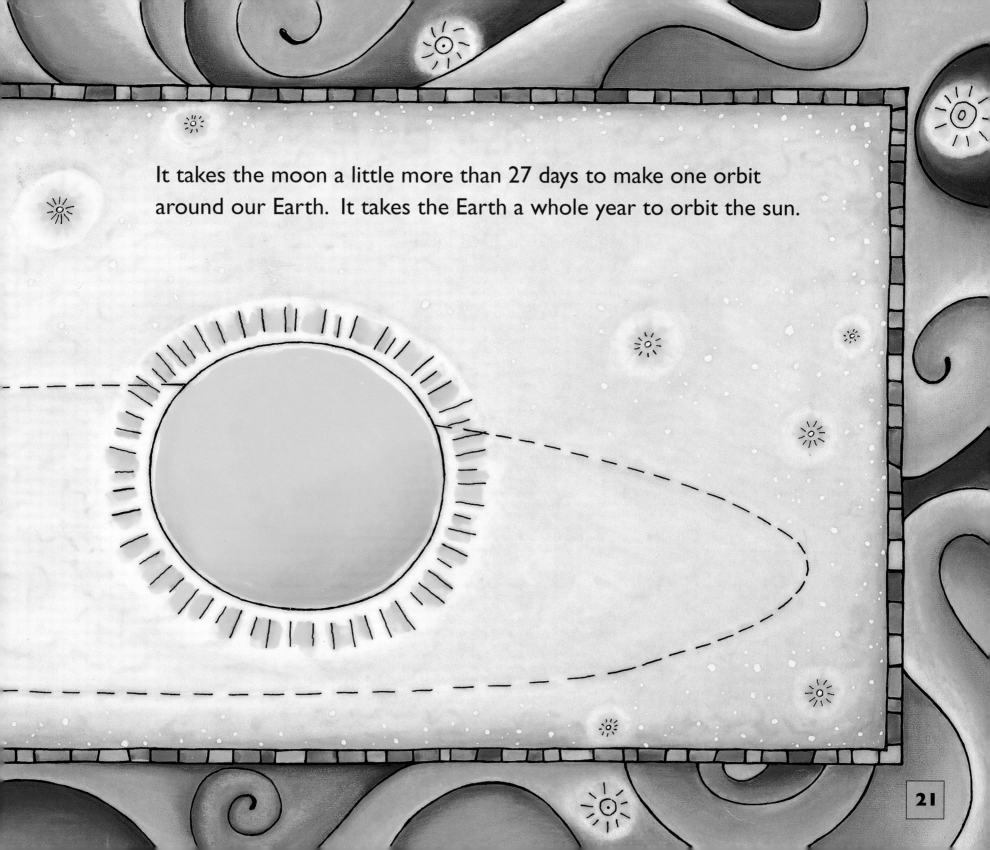

It takes the moon a little more than 27 days to make one orbit around our Earth. It takes the Earth a whole year to orbit the sun.

One side of the moon is always facing away from the Earth. For years, no one on Earth had been able to see the "far side" of the moon. Then a spacecraft from the Soviet Union flew around the moon and took pictures of it. The pictures showed that the far side had many more small craters but fewer "seas" than the side of the moon we see from Earth.

Just like the Earth, the moon gets all of its light from the sun. We see the moon because light from the sun hits the moon and bounces off. Light reflects off the moon, just like it does off a mirror. If the moon did not reflect the sun's light, we would not be able to see it.

One side of the moon is always being lit by the sun. Because of the way the moon moves, sometimes we only see a small piece of the lit side. On these days the moon looks like a skinny little banana. Scientists call this shape the crescent moon.

Sometimes we see the whole lit side of the moon. That's when the moon looks big and round like a giant beach ball. Scientists call this shape the full moon. If you watch carefully, you'll see that the moon will look like it changes its shape a little every night. When this happens, we say the moon is going through phases.

On July 20, 1969, an American spacecraft called Apollo 11 landed on the moon. On that day astronauts Neil Armstrong and Edwin "Buzz" Aldrin became the first people to walk on the moon. The moon has no air. They had to wear special suits to protect them when they walked on the lunar surface.

When astronauts Armstrong and Aldrin first stepped onto the moon, they didn't know what to expect. They found out that the surface of the moon is covered in fine dust, almost like flour. From 1969 to 1972, twelve different astronauts were able to visit the moon. They left footprints on the moon that are still there today.

The moon is our companion in space. We don't go anywhere without it. From Earth, the moon looks like a big white ball. From the moon, the astronauts could see that our Earth was a special place.' It was full of color and life, and there was nothing else like it in the sky.

Someday, people may go back to the moon. We may even set up a place there where people can live and work. Until we do, we can all visit the moon just by looking at it. Maybe if you're lucky, you too will travel to the moon.

Making Craters

Try making your own model craters on a lunar landscape.

Here's What You'll Need:

 A large metal cake pan or baking dish

 A sheet of old newspaper

 Several cups of white flour

 5 pebbles that are slightly different sizes

 A ruler

1 Spread the newspaper across a table. Place the metal pan in the middle.

2 Fill the pan with flour so that it's about 1 inch deep. Smooth it out by shaking the pan gently.

3 Take the first pebble and hold it about 2 feet above the pan of flour.

4 Drop the pebble into the flour and watch what happens.

5 Repeat step 4 with the other pebbles.

What happens to the flour when the pebble hits the surface?

How does this experiment explain how craters form?

Were there any differences in the sizes of the craters?

What did you discover?

When the pebble hit the flour, the flour flew out of the way and made a crater. Bigger pebbles made bigger craters. In this experiment, the pebbles acted like meteorites hitting the surface of the moon. From this experiment you can see that the very large craters on the moon had to have been made by very large meteorites.

Use a mirror to read!

When the made a cr

Book design by Susan Kehnemui Donnelly.
The text is set in Gill Sans.
The display type is Dollhouse and Tree-Boxelder.

Jump Into Science™ series consultant: Christine Kiel, Early Education
Science Specialist

The Author warmly thanks Mr. John Farina, amateur astronomer
extraordinaire, for all his suggestions and guidance in putting
together this manuscript.

Library of Congress Cataloging-in-Publication Data

Tomecek, Steve.
  Moon / by Steve Tomecek ; illustrated by Liisa Chauncy Guida.
    p. cm. — (Jump into science)
  Trade Edition ISBN 0-7922-5123-7, Library Edition ISBN 0-7922-8304-X
  1. Moon—Juvenile literature. I. Guida, Liisa Chauncy. II. Title. III. Series.
  QB52.T64 2004
  523.3—dc22
                                    2004008761

One of the world's largest nonprofit scientific and educational
organizations, the National Geographic Society was founded in 1888
"for the increase and diffusion of geographic knowledge." Fulfilling this
mission, the Society educates and inspires millions every day through
its magazines, books, television programs, videos, maps and atlases,
research grants, the National Geographic Bee, teacher workshops, and
innovative classroom materials. The Society is supported through
membership dues, charitable gifts, and income from the sale of its
educational products. This support is vital to National Geographic's
mission to increase global understanding and promote conservation of
our planet through exploration, research, and education.

For more information, please call 1-800-NGS LINE (647-5463) or
write to the following address:

NATIONAL GEOGRAPHIC SOCIETY
1145 17th Street N.W.
Washington, D.C. 20036-4688 U.S.A.

Visit the Society's Web site at www.nationalgeographic.com.

Printed in the United States of America